Waterfront Reveries

Poems by
William Cipriano

Introduction and Arrangement by Jeri Cipriano

gatekeeper press
Columbus, Ohio

Waterfront Reveries
Poems by William Cipriano

Published by Gatekeeper Press
2167 Stringtown Rd, Suite 109
Columbus, OH 43123-2989
www.GatekeeperPress.com

The editorial work for this book is entirely the product of the author and the copyright holder. Gatekeeper Press did not participate in and is not responsible for any aspect of this element.

Cover Image: iStockphoto.com/MichaelVerSprill (Golden Ripples in the Hudson River)

ISBN (paperback): 9781662930973

For Rachel and Marcello

INTRODUCTION

For as long as I knew him (and before), Bill was always writing, especially poems. His knowledge of poetry as a genre — its forms and its masters — was extensive. He refers to some in his poems.

This book contains all his collected poems, intertwined and grouped by theme. In early ones, he employs irony and humor to craft a certain "persona"; in later ones, he speaks more from the heart.

As a therapist and by nature, Bill brought people together. I do believe he left his body of work as a means through which all who loved him could stay connected. The poems live on the pages; Bill's life and personhood, in our hearts and minds.

Before she died, "Oma" (Bill's mother) said she had two sons: one who healed bodies and the other who healed souls. Bill's quick retort was, "Do we have another brother you never told us about?"

Bill had a wry sense of humor, which is why I think he would have appreciated the following quote purported to be uttered by Beethoven on his deathbed:

"Applaud, my friends, the comedy is over."

—Jeri Cipriano
With love and gratitude

CONTENTS

PROLOGUE

Show Time

Hands deep inside the pockets of his coat,
the poet stands alone among the crowd and waits
for the slightest provocation,
the merest chance
to expose his poem.

WILLIAM ADVISES

A Design Glitch

Smooth the edges and miter the corners.
Plumb the joists true.
Level the crossbeams square.
Put braces front and back.
Use glue and nails and lots of screws.
Bolt contact points to steady ground.
(One cannot be too sure.)
Then settle back
and hum a tune
and watch it dance.

At End Of Term

The students gathered to express concern.

Given nuclear proliferation,
the Middle East crisis,
startling breakthroughs in genetic research,
the Trump presidency,
global warming,
and toxic waste,
did I think the world would last much longer?

After some consideration,
I assured them,
with every certainty,
the final exam,
essay questions only,
would be held in the hall assigned for that purpose,
on the determined date,
as forecast in the syllabus.

Note to the Faculty

This place is parched.
Everything snaps and cracks.
The rain that comes with joy and sadness
falls elsewhere.

What laws do we defy,
living only by tensor light?
And what are we growing?

Rerun

Hit the beachhead chin first.
Forget the sand.
Keep your eyes front and weapon pointed straight ahead.
Adjust your balls.
Consider the territory hostile.
Lay down fire.
Stop only when smart to do so.
War sucks.
Ignore the news.
Remember the mission,
the mission and the squad.
You need the squad.
The squad needs you to complete the mission.
Stay connected.
No one survives alone,
except in bad movies.
Either you take it in the shorts,
which everyone expects,
or else you don't,
which nobody believes.
Only your mother cares.
Besides,
It's none of your business.
Only keep your eyes front and weapon pointed straight ahead
and your balls adjusted.

To Keats

Dear John,

In your absence, some things have changed;
namely,
truth is now spin,
spin truth;
beauty, self-expression;
self-expression, beauty.

That's it.
That's all.

. . . just an update.

. . . no reason to reply.

Until I bring you better news,
stay put.

Yours,
Bill

Words For Old Age

Keep all parts moist
except the eyes,
and flexible
except the will.

WILLIAM'S APHORISMS

Not warmth . . . accuracy.

. . . .

Money is its own reward.

. . . .

Life doesn't want a note from the doctor.

. . . .

Do not bite the ass that feeds you.

. . . .

Consider fair
everything between first and
third base.

. . . .

Those who refuse to blink
won't see
when the time comes.

. . . .

If you aren't laughing,
you really don't understand the situation.

WILLIAM ON AGING

As Matters Stand

Not much of me works anymore.
Everything hurts.
Parts throb.
I can't walk without pain
or lift my arms.
I depend on the kindness of strangers for little things,
me, a gladiator,
a warrior in the endless fight against ignorance,
superstition,
and growing old;
me, who won't surrender.

Of course,
I expect matters to get worse,
but for right now,
part of me is grateful.
I've never felt so close to death,
so hopelessly alive,
so tethered to the earth,
and you.

"Mirror, Mirror ..."

Receding gums,
a grizzled pate,
watery eyes,
two weary jowls,
simian ears,
three liver spots,
a rumpled face.

What price experience!
. . . wisdom?
That's another matter.

At Thirty-Six
For My Treasure

I never planned to live this long,
weak and surrounded by pills,
short of breath, half helpless,
but someone has to round the curve.
Not everyone enters old age upright.

I take life as it comes
and try not to complain,
try not to want too much.
I've outlived my measure.
My mother taught me gratitude.

I don't believe in any afterlife,
certainly not heaven.
I believe in now, the moment,
if I believe in anything at all.
At my age, I keep the horizon close.

In the morning, I open my eyes, and surprise!
I'm here and you are there beside me once again,
and all I want, all that matters, I can hold
for as long as it lasts.

It makes a guy want to hang around a little longer.

Ballad of a Troubadour Past Fifty

The high notes never did ring out,
and the pipes get thicker with age,
Now, breathing has become more difficult,
but even before that,
the sense of line,
the exquisite urgency that joins the end to the beginning
of things
got lost,
and, frankly, too,
my arms ache holding this guitar,
holding this guitar and standing,
standing every night beneath your window,
standing, Lady,
standing;
standing hurts my back.

Change Of Address

Nothing matters in the long run
where I lived once,
in the long run,
trying to make sense of the past,
find hope for the future.
Lately,
I live in the short run,
right now,
nursing my arthritis,
counting pain pills,
trying to help out where I can,
doing small stuff,
taking it slow.

I took quite a while getting here.
Of course,
I had no sense of direction,
the landmarks kept disappearing,
road signs made no sense,
and, frankly, I didn't always pay attention.
But now that I've arrived,
I belong here,
asking only questions that have answers,
owning what I can own,
doing what's on my to-do list,
being . . .
mostly being,
taking in all kinds of weather gladly,
reaching out where I can,
living within limits,
and learning not to push.
I revise history my way now.
The future has always been on its own.

In Late Autumn

The sun hangs tough before it sets,
never looks more beautiful than in final light,
the colors of fire,
as we watch from the deck,
silent,
we two,
day's duties done.
I pour a wine
or you . . .

In time,
everything disappears.
Friends go.
The kids leave one by one,
and the dog limps from room to room,
but we remain,
for a while anyway,
to banter and bicker,
teeter and cling,
then only you
or maybe me.

Here . . . sit closer.
Is there still much to say?
Tell me.
There to the west . . .
The sun has not yet given up,
and wine does not stay chilled forever.

In My Garden

From my chair
I can see the dogwood blooming,
fragile in pink and white;
the brave dogwood knowing it won't last.
The forsythia have already gone.
The deer ate the tulips.
Will the tulips return again next year?
The deer surely.
Daffodils remain stalwart,
defiant in cautionary yellow.
Good for the daffodils, I say,
and me.
Lacking much else,
I rely on nature to get me through.
Seasons return and all that stuff,
but I'm not fooled.
Someday I won't return.
So much for nature.
I feel like the dogwood when the bloom has fallen.
And the options?
I guess I can hang with daffodils,
until tomorrow anyway.
I'm still waiting for the roses.
Roses have thorns.

Night Song At Seventy

By early light,
I leave the comfort of your warmth
and rush wordless into traffic while you abide,
O keeper of my soul.
We go separate ways on common missions,
staying in touch without touching.

Necessity dictates,
I know.

By amber light,
we meet again,
dine across from one another,
watch television side-by-side,
stay close in separate rooms.

Do not misunderstand.
We do well together apart.
You are always quite near.

But by nightfall, I ache.
I ache to feel the rhythm of your heart against my chest,
the stillness of your skin on mine.

Let me hold you.

Nights pass quickly,
and we have so few left.

Now We Are 82
(after Milne)

Long since begun
and hardly new,
I'm all grown up,
now 82.
Finally me,
and still very clever.
Could I be 82
forever and ever?

William Goes Gentle
Into That Good Night
(after Thomas)

They flood the ads:
old people selling deception,
swimming in azure waters,
running on coral sands,
dancing all night,
falling in love again for the first time,
denying joint pain,
memory loss,
the inevitable.

William admires their endless smiles,
quaint enthusiasm,
and poor arithmetic.
("At sixty, I have my whole life ahead of me," says one.)

William has come lately, fit from the wars.
Scars adorn his soul.
He wears his liver spots with pride.
He limps.
He squints to hear.
He has raised his children,
served his country,
and always worked two jobs.
He has already done the azure-waters-coral-sands thing,
has fallen in love just the right number of times,
and doesn't dance.

Now at some venerable age,
he chooses to behave venerably,
to sit by the Hudson,
next to her without whom nothing makes sense,
and listen to the stillness of the river,
while a soft breeze flushes his bones
until it doesn't anymore.
Still, if needed,
he remains on call.

He can be found under some trees
closest to the river.
Just show up, and bring wine,
a cheap malbec will do
unfashionably chilled.

William Struggles For Position
(after Bukowski)

The Dewar's gone,
William hugs the carpet,
sure of his gift,
and spent
as usual,
having just given life
another six percent of all he's got.

Each night,
he huddles there in the same spot,
to avoid crowds,
writes poems to himself,
throws up,
closes his eyes,
hums the *vissi d'arte* from *Tosca*,
pees in his pants warmly,
smiling,
as only someone can
who knows the full extent
of the world's loss.

Words for a Cane

Balance, Good Friend,
you bring balance to a life off-kilter,
assurance in an unsure world.
We should have met sooner,
when I lived in constant fear of falling.
Now, thanks to you,
I move around bravely,
with one foot firmly planted in reality,
as has been suggested,
assured, however, but never quite satisfied,
vexed by the need to go places.
On occasion, I cry "Forward!"
brandishing you, O Cane,
(as you may have noticed).
Still, to go where, I ask,
Do what?
. . . someplace warm, yes,
that keeps me from doing mischief, of course,
but so many places are warm,
and I can manage mischief anywhere,
so I stay here by you, O Cane,
with one foot firmly planted in reality,
as has been suggested,
going no place special,
just around and around,
and around and around,
bravely,
balanced,
and in the groove.

WILLIAM ON DYING

An Accounting Concern

Since I expect nothing from life,
asking for anything seems out of place.
Even something simple
like "Kindly pass the salt,"
I have trouble saying.
Pass it?
I always do when asked,
but ask myself?
Never.
I'd rather wait until the salt arrives
down at my end of the table,
and if it never does,
I'll eat flat food,
and not for the first time, either.
More than enjoy dinner,
I want to die debt-free.
That won't happen,
but at least now,
come Judgment Day,
I won't owe anybody salt.

The Day My Mother Died

The day my mother died,
I became the boy in the photo on the table by her bed,
standing like a soldier in high-top shoes,
all knees and crooked bangs and bucket ears,
looking out wide-behind-the-eyes
at an unavailable world,
wanting to hold my mother's hand,
to hear her tell me one more time
what makes the sky blue.

Autumn Poem

In fall,
before the final frost,
a passion rages red and gold along a
weary landscape,
an unrequited passion, true,
but bold.
Even leaves grown worn and old,
have fire left to warm the cold.

Confrontation

He showed up unannounced,
an intruder, really,
black and beady,
from who-knows-where,
through what hole in the home's defense,
curled on the couch downstairs in front of the television,
hiding in his own fur,
eyes rolling back,
more scared of me than me of him,
a raccoon or something,
wanting a quiet place to die.

. . . simple,
a small enough demand,
but I could not have that,
not me.
These creatures bring pestilence,
and one can never be too sure.
So I just put a bullet in his head
. . . one shot.

. . . a little guy
who just wanted a quiet place to die.

. . . better for him, I tell myself,
maybe,
but not for me.

Graveside

Thanks for coming.
I am not here
(as you may have noticed).
I am below
(or will be soon),
boxed in the fatal earth
where I expect to rot
(. . . don't know about the box).
Heaven and Hell do not figure in my cosmology,
so I'm here into perpetuity,
just about where you're standing.

I tell you this,
so you will not look for me elsewhere
among the stars, for example,
or listen for me in the wind.
I will not become a river
or a field of poppies,
or anything sylvan.

If I continue to exist,
it will be in your thoughts
and, maybe, if you say my name,
in the thoughts of those who follow,
until you and they can no longer remember.
Then I will be just a name in some registry.

Obituary for a Friend

Nothing rises up anymore,
towers in priapic glory.
The Frightful One is dead,
lying where he's always lived,
shriveled like a frightened turtle,
his powers gone.
Long live the Frightful One!
He only wanted to be accepted,
thought of fondly.
Women who knew him mourn their loss,
as do women who only heard his name.
Everyone agrees, however.
The neighborhood is safer.
As for me,
I'm free
at last.

Staying In Touch
(for Rachel)

My daughter is on a mission.
Ill as I am,
and expecting the worst,
she would have me use signs
to reach her from the other side.
She believes in that stuff —
that, and news from the stars.
I don't argue,
Ill as I am,
and completely out of my depth,
I don't want to disappoint her.
I thought when she saw a rainbow
she might know I am there,
but somebody already took rainbows.
I went through white dogs and roses,
the national anthem, and different foods.
I exhausted the name of novels, flowers, fruit, films, symphonies,
and anything random,
until I could no longer think.
Then I hit on at least one sign:
When she sees a mushroom,
she should remember how it's grown,
shrouded in darkness,
and covered with shit,
and know I am with her,
and that everything's fine.

Tell The Doctors

When near the end,
skip all the magical thinking.
Don't plead for extra time on my behalf.
I had my run.
Rather,
tell the doctors to forget their needles, tubes, and scalpels,
their potions meant to salvage hopeless lives.
Instead,
tell them to set a table rich with food and drink,
and seat my friends and family all around,
locked in mortal conversation,
screaming at each other,
laughing,
crying,
fighting,
hugging,
singing,
dancing to music that won't stop,
and prop me up.
Maybe I'll be around when the kitchen closes
and everyone has left.
Maybe I won't.
In any case,
tell the doctors to go easy on the morphine.
When near the end,
I want to be alive,
Not just living.

To Joggers Who Make Much of Time
(Not to Mention Distance)
(after Marvel)

Gravity ruled by the moon pushes back the seas
and pulls the belly past the belt,
the chin onto the chest,
the lids over the eyes,
the flesh into the grave, no more to rise
(except now and then in parts of California);
therefore,
relax the muscles of the face.
Everyone crosses the finish line sooner or later,
collects the same chill prize.

Just remember,
at the penultimate moment,
say "Thanks."

William Goes Underground
(after Dostoyevsky/Bukowski)

Let William die incorrectly,
at public cost,
with much back and forth to the hospital.
Let tubes man every orifice
while doctors grouse,
and William stares into the void.

And then,
when his time comes,
plant the miserable bastard,
each hair and bone,
anywhere in the way,
where developers plan a mall;
city fathers, a parking lot,
something reasonable and efficient,
all for the God-damn common good,
and mark the spot,
a monument to spite,
everything awkward, rude, bitter,
human for its own sake, and free,
in memory of him and you and me
and all of us.

WILLIAM ON FATHERHOOD

Father Poem

(1)

Father is a child of the Depression.
He said so every day:
"I'm a child of the Depression," he said.

Father said the Depression was very sad.
There was no work.
There was no food.
There was no place to sleep.

Father said it's hard to be a child of the Depression.
I know it's hard to be a child of a child of the Depression.

(2)

My father's suits had always been too small,
too tight in the shoulders,
too narrow in the rise.

Still, I wore them like a dutiful son
while Father waited anxiously
for them to fit.

(3)

For yet another year,
The GDP had fallen short of hopes.
From my window,
I heard Father in our garden urging all the plants to be more
useful.
"Be more useful," he urged.
When, finally, he pulled them out, I left
to root and grow again
where there was oxygen.

(4)

Far from my father's voice,
commitments met,
I clawed my collar,
for something else,
for something more,
something.

(5)

Friends say I've changed,
who no longer find socks inside the couch,
underwear down the hall.

Now I file everything away,
in rust-brown envelopes with string,
just like the ones
that brought my father peace of mind.

(6)

"Good luck," my father said,
casually,
curled in bed while cancer ate his liver,
and I walked out the door.
He died,
quite out of character,
without waiting for my return.

(7)

The GDP continues down,
and my father,
in another garden these days,
just urges all the plants,
simply
to be.

First Meeting

Life seemed all right
until that summer afternoon
when Father shaved,
without warning;
just hacked away
that fierce, black underbrush
beneath his nose.

My child's eyes stared bereft.

Father smiled for the first time in his life,
as I ran from the room.

Years passed
while I learned to know my father again.

From a Book of Half-Hours
(after Rilke)

(1)

. . . ran into S
who still finds you fiction,
but, nonetheless,
blames you for the misery of the world,
everything, everywhere,
ever.

S still prefers the Great Socialist State,
long lines,
official stamps,
equally empty bins,
benefitting everybody,
of course.

". . . not for me," I told him.
I have always found Paradise someone else's idea.

Personally,
I've grown accustomed to the random way you screw things
up.

Besides, I loathe standing in line.

(2)

. . . just returned from temple
where, as always,
we praised your name,

stood up,
sat down,
and did the you're-so-big-I'm-so-small thing
during which time I ask myself:
What sort of guy wants people to do this?
Have you no modesty?
But, no matter,
don't ask me why.
Around this time next year,
I'll be sitting in the same place,
behind the family with the lame child
who talks through silent prayer.

(3)

A Christmas letter came this year
from one of your people
extending to me "the Son's eternal promise."

Needless to say,
my gratitude abounds;
nevertheless,
I've had enough of promises.

I hope you understand.

Besides,
nothing goes on forever,
even under celestial conditions,
or sounds all that appealing.

Instead,
without seeming pushy,
could I get a break or two here and now,

or tomorrow, at the latest?
Anything small will do.
No promises.
Surprise me! Make my day!

(4)

. . . and on the matter of my being your servant:
Who thought of that?
You ought to know by now
I don't beseech too well.
"Take it or leave it," has always been my motto,
and "What you see is what you get."
But did you ask?

All of which brings me to another point:
Have you given our relationship any thought?
Doesn't it seem one-sided to you?

(5)

As a father,
you deal hands-off,
write lists of "Don'ts,"
stand back,
watch your children fall down,
get up,
fall down,
get up,
throw sand,
smash each other's castles,
each other's skulls.
Then you visit them with locusts, floods, and boils.

What's that supposed to do?
Over millennia, what's changed?
Has anyone learned anything?
Instead,
your children spend a lot of time confused,
pissed off, frankly.
The way you do things makes problems.
Have you considered positive reinforcement?
In any case,
may I suggest you get some help.
The local library holds a parenting skills workshop
the final Wednesday of each month,
open to the public,
attendance free.

(6)

On second thought,
just leave us alone.

Lesson

"Life's serious business," said my father seriously,
to which my mother added, looking directly at me,
"So, you, stop with the jokes."
My father could not keep from telling jokes.
My mother could not help but laugh at them.

William Watching His Daughter Stand for the First Time

The need to pull oneself erect,
equals only
the struggle to stay that way.

WILLIAM ON HONOR

A Hero For Our Time

Given a choice,
I would rather have been Hector,
noble Hector,
abandoned by the gods
and doomed to die in a lost cause;
Hector,
who fought bravely knowing his fate,
unlike myself
who is just doomed.

I had not planned for this:
to strut around suburbia,
helmet gleaming,
armor polished,
sword drawn,
looking for Achilles,
but duty calls.
People just look at me
as I pursue honor.

Honor is hard to pursue here,
Shielded by privately-owned trees,
but I'm pretty sure no one will cut out my guts.
The fight for tax relief,
faster snow removal,

and better schools
requires stamina,
not heroics.

On the plus side,
there's not much chance
of victorious enemies
dragging my corpse around the village
behind a horse.

That would really upset the kids.

Call To Duty

Hear ye! Hear ye!
Know that William,
ever ready,
and equipped as always,
with limited vision,
small wit,
the truth as he sees it,
and an endless list of good intentions,
prepares, once and for all,
to make the world a better place.

See him in full armor,
mounted,
sword drawn,
stead high,
steady,
plume proud
ready,
ever ready.

Plus C'est La Même Chose

The heroes all have gone,
died, fled, or surrendered,
leaving us to ourselves,
we two,
with no ammo,
cover,
or much to drink.
Meanwhile, the Shits advance,
as the Shits always do.
History tells us
the weather promises to be ugly,
even in spring,
but not to fret.
We have been here before.
Then, we broke out the beer and sausages
and waited for help to arrive.
Maybe this time,
while waiting, we can read
or listen to music,
the music of the spheres
(. . . not the same since Schoenberg, I know).
Of course,
we can still dance.
I'll lead,
then you,
or better yet,
just twist and shout.

Tribute

Thank you,
John Wayne,
for once again,
saving
Kansas.

William's Last Words

Tell them I was there.
Tell them I was there and threw my sword aside and stood,
barehanded and alone, in the open field with the wind
and the rain,
ready.
Tell them that,
and that I waited,
but no one came.

WILLIAM ON LOVE

Aubade
(after Williams)

You never look more beautiful
than when the sun wakes up.
With startled hair and rumpled face,
you open up heavy eyes
and say "Hello,"
to me, of all people.

Before you put a brush to anything,
meet me in the kitchen
and kiss me with your morning mouth.
I'll make the coffee.

Counting the Ways at Twenty-Eight
For My Treasure

. . . no great subject for poetry
or art;
nothing unusual
or deep.

One night,
at a party,
out of nowhere,
a girl appeared in a doorway,
and this guy swore right then,
not to let her out of his sight,
and never did,
ever.

. . . not much to tell
really.

For Max

How magnificent a creature!
How taut his frame!
How majestic —
head high,
eyes front,
god-like,
cousin to the wolf,
defender of the hearth,
master of his domain.
One who eats heartily
and sleeps justly,
knowing each day
that he played his very best game
and owes the world nothing.
A paragon of loyalty,
a model of virtue,
all managed with a brain
the size of a walnut.

Last Love Poem

There's no way left, Dear Heart, to prove
my love.
I would have given you the moon,
but others got there first,
and who wants such a gift
with footprints on it.

Lusty Pirate William

By dark,
William,
that wily buccaneer,
plunders his own,
scouts his wife's hip over the curve upward,
across the shoulder to the neck,
then down the front,
along the breast gently,
pauses,
drops suddenly to the belly,
then lower still
to find such treasure not quite hidden by her thighs
to make all nature blush
that once belonged
to lots of other guys.

March Exercise

An empty park . . .
Forsythia . . .
Moss on a black stone wall . . .
Bare roots and barren trees . . .
Mud and puddles . . .
Sun working at a lifeless sky . . .
Raw wind whipping across the Hudson . . .
Jersey in the background
and, in the foreground — you.

Max: In Memoriam

His ashes sit in a blank box
on the mantel behind a vase
without flowers.

I need him near.

Max lacked a moral code,
believed in no one's gods,
missed the finer points of language.
Deceit, he never understood,
and so,
lived each moment straight up,
flat out,
open,
with neither irony nor shame.

He reminds me.

Others remind me, too.
"Dogs just want food."
Maybe they do.
"You'll get over it," friends tell me.

Maybe I will,
but they did not know him.

One More For Max

55

Keep close, Good Friend,
so I can watch,
and maybe learn
to breathe the air each day for the first
time,
frolic,
forgive,
and always tell the truth.

Three Sonnets
For Jeri

(1)

What exercise did English past contrive
for love with rhymes and ending couplets hung
on quatrains three of measured iambs five,
to trick the heart, the mind, dismay the tongue?

If Sydney, Johnson, Spenser honed the art,
their songs bring yawns and moans more times than not.
The form would cripple reasons of the heart
and lead to poets fudging lines a lot.

Italians brought the English small relief
with eight plus six instead of three times four
plus two, but linger in the quaint belief
that passion counts, but numbers matter more.

Such are the rules by which I must abide
for you, my Love, to prove both true and tried.

(2)

Consider what's about to happen now
and how the letters falter on the page,
and think about the sweat, the knitted brow
and how the mood divides 'twixt love and rage.

Consider love and rage and in-between
how language cannot grasp the subtle pale,
and know how hard each word must work to mean
and how, regardless, words are doomed to fail.

Consider in the end that love is mute,
a silent longing pleading in the void,
that brings my senses to their most acute,
and only leaves me hopelessly annoyed.

Consider, too, that I would hold you near
and how my arms alone can make that clear.

(3)

Beware the sanctimonious or worse,
the plain, well-meaning legislating good,
and poets wailing sentimental verse
to make themselves feel better than they should.

Beware, above all, language vague, words vast
like "freedom," "love," and "truth," and so much more
that brought on endless trouble in the past
and left the world in constant states of war.

"Love" more than "truth," of these is most suspect
which oozes boundless, leaks into the soul.
The heart reacts. The mind cannot reflect,
a helpless body then yields up the whole.

So always check me when I get verbose.
Regard my hands and parse each sentence close.

Unmanaged Care

Once in a while,
a new and improved marriage comes along,
enriched,
with instructions on what to do and how to be:
"Have date night once a week."
Fridays seem popular.
"Monitor what you say."
Stay with "I"-messages.
"Put yourself in the other's place."
Exchange roles.

Myself,
I like the old, messy marriage,
 unkempt
with just enough anger and frustration,
just enough misunderstanding
for a proper, vital marriage
of two souls in combat,
resisting fate,
ruled by the heart,
helpless and real,
where all can be forgiven with a hug,
a look,
or a mumbled regret,
knowing the hug will be returned,
the look understood,
the words accepted,
knowing
time after time
and for every time after that,
knowing.

William Atones

Go ahead, turn away.
Nothing says more than a bare back.
Pull the covers over your head.
Review the day.
Chew each injustice thoroughly.
Above all, seethe.

Just know,
William accused
always sides with those who grieve against him,
pleads no contest.
He stands with you.

How about a glass of water?

. . . a glass of water from the refrigerator?

. . . Colorado?

. . . Lourdes, perhaps?

Know, too, William abides
even where he disturbs.

Oh, Lady, please,
William mistrusts language,
but not the heart,
does vodka by the fifth,
can't sing,
write a sonnet,
or cross the street without a choreographer.

A sign would help.

How about an arm offered carefully?

. . . a foot?

The direct route would be flat rejection,
but uncertainty also works.

How about a nightmare
just between us?

WILLIAM OBSERVES

At The Symposium

Over white wine and fish ovum,
the critics gather to discuss
"Toward an Understanding of a Marxist Jungian Analysis of the
Deconstructed Symbolism in the Works of Post-Vietnam-War
Women Writers of the Minimalist School as It Concerns Feminist
Archetypes,"
a topic of great concern.
Much to debate.
Passions run high.
Positions are stated,
alliances formed and reformed,
friendships broken.
The gathering runs overtime.
People leave, avoiding one another.
The next symposium will be a month from now.

Meanwhile,
two acquaintances meet,
coming from the library,
books in hand.
They talk
and realize they're carrying the same novel.
"Did you read the second paragraph on page 154?"

They read the passage in silence,
then look up.
"Beautiful."
"Beautiful."
"The part where he realizes she's gone."
"The part where he realizes she's gone."
They smile and start to walk.
It is evening and spring.
"A beer? Coffee?"
"A beer."
On the way, they discuss last night's Mets-Phillies game.

Bent Branch

Given their positions on the phylogenetic tree,
the guinea pig should clean out William's cage.

Curriculum Vitae

A plant sat on my windowsill,
grew old,
and died.
Wanted water now and then,
and, in its time, a little light,
but nothing more.
Was always beautiful,
of far more use just so
then I shall ever be
and never needed a psychiatrist.

Commencement Address
(after Shakespeare/Hopkins)

Go forth!
Go forth in existential May!
Find authenticity and bliss.
Settle for nothing less than both.
Maintain integrity.
The purity is all,
and bliss.
Don't forget bliss.
Throw yourself on the winds of chance bravely.
The risk is all.
Conserve.
Create.
Yes, conserve and create.
Of course, "to thine own self be true,"
and then get over it.
(You have more than one self.)
Go forth!
Find love.
Let love find you.
Be open.
The openness is all,
and then, when you and love find each other,
forget all previous advice.
Put dreams aside.
Keep love alive no matter what.
Be generous.
The generosity is all.
Get soiled without shame, regret, or feelings of failure.
Tread carefully.
So much depends on you,

and look beyond yourself,
as did once in Majorca, Brother Alfonso
who only watched the door,
so others could go forth.

Going Places

Most people like to know where they're going,
read the brochures,
find what's recommended,
make plans,
and book ahead.

Most people like everything as ordered,
just so,
promptly,
smiling,
in soft comfort.

Most people like to disembark,
guidebook in hand,
prepared,
in the warm glow
of the merely probable.

Heartland

Nothing reaches up here.
Everything just lays back,
you know,
nice and easy,
and just spreads out,
around drive-in mortuaries,
Taco Bells and motels,
trailer parks and billboards,
and shit like that,
and friendly-like,
you know,
sort of blisters,
freezes over,
and floods.

History

Western civilization has always confused
ease with progress,
comfort with happiness.

Irony

Irony smiles at tragedy,
but does not mock;
respects its truth,
simply sees the need to keep on going,
knowing.

Progress

The quarters drop.
. . . no change,
and once again,
HOTWHIPPEDEXTRABLACKCOFFEECREAM
Any time you want it.

Referendum

New Jersey decided to widen its people,
but the parkways complained.
Now traffic moves in monotone
on highways leading to Bayonne.

Still Life

At four ninety-nine a pound,
they seemed so unapproachable,
true spheres in a world slightly flattened on one end,
in a fading city.
Splashes of chromium yellow,
splattered crimson,
washed rose,
amber at the edges,
flawless,
taut, peach on peach
in a frail, perfect
pyramid.

Even chilled, they tasted,
felt like,
oatmeal.

The Gathering

Deer gather on the lawn.
They eat my hosta.
Why not? It's there.
I planted it,
but maybe it belongs to them.
They were here first.
I'm the intruder, with my ranch-style house,
complete with central air-conditioning
and asphalt driveway extra-wide.
I'm the stranger
who pushed them from their home.
Still, they seem so content,
with their little jaws moving side to side.
I'd like to join them.
I wonder if they'd mind.

Thoughts in Bad Weather

The night is dark and long,
the rain cold, hard,
the wind, ragged.

How long can the battlements hold?

I pull the blankets up around my neck,
sink further into bed,
listen to the windows shudder,
and wonder how the homeless are doing.
Have the deer who eat my garden taken refuge,
and all the feral cats
that roam the railroad tracks?
I wonder if the creatures who make furrows in my lawn
can find a place to hide.
Is all my family safe?
Are the buried dead warm and dry?

True Believer

He could not manage the shadows,
stumbled,
and wandered off.
He needed to see perfectly,
needed white lines on a black street
so he could find his way —
the right,
the only way,
when, all at once, he saw a slice of light
and grabbed,
and held tight
with all his might,
and absolutely sure,
secure,
and wholly pure,
he choked the sun.

While Pulling Weeds

This can't be right.
Where do I get off deciding what lives or dies,
disfiguring some grand design?
Who made this a worthwhile project?
Let the fittest survive, I say.
Nature knows best,
as I bend in the morning sun,
sweat dripping in my eyes.

Besides,
these unruly plants bring something sudden to their fixed world.
Fighting for position,
they violate boundaries,
intrude between roses and azaleas,
azaleas and hydrangeas and hydrangeas and everything else
choking
their available world until, all at once, they blossom,
defiantly,
in colors unapproved,
or just stand there in the wrong place
vital and relentless.

Unruly once myself,
no one pulled me.

The garden looked better
before I showed up.

WILLIAM ON POESY

Ars Poetica

A poem isn't like a bench
on which to stand
to reason or to preach.

It's more like a pillow
to bolster the head for comfort,
the butt
for ease.

Pragmaticus Poeticus

A poem ought to mean and be,
or not,
and doing so,
should make somebody laugh
or cry,
or linger on the edge of both
bravely.

Otherwise, who needs one?
The world already has too many words to read.

A poem ought to happen by surprise
between the kishkes
and the funny bone,
or just fester.

Rainfall
(after Hopkins)

Outside,
a benevolent rain
falls on a grateful Earth,
nurturing the plants and flowers.
From my study,
strewn with rumpled thoughts,
I watch them grow
until they come alive in vibrant colors,
their full potential realized.
I watch
and wait
for rain to fall
inside.

Rules For Writing Great Poetry

Enter sober,
bent by the weight of heavy themes:
aging,
death, dying,
the void.
Love's always good for a sonnet;
courage, for just a few stanzas.
Don't push.
Be grave.
The gravity is all,
and sen-si-ti-vi-ty.
Be sen-si-tive.
Most of all, rage.
Rage against this and that, and nothing.
Just rage.
Readers identify with rage.
Don't forget the seasons, either, and how they come and go.
And show respect,
For in the end,
words fail, so
be obscure.
No one knows what's going on anyway.
Let emotions depart freely from tranquility,
but not as to disturb anyone.
Most people don't like being moved.
It's too moving.

State of the Art

Forget memorable language,
taut and unexpected,
or the urgency of felt needs,
the need to make you see.

Complexity is all,
the forced image,
the contrived metaphor,
edginess for its own sake.

Only make the poem
a rubric cube of words
to overwork the brain,
while the heart goes unattended
(not to mention, the funny bone).

WILLIAM ON WILLIAM

After Listening to the Last Act of Boito's Mefistofele

Except for such moments,
William,
gladly,
would have been a turtle.

"I Do"

I have bad breath.

I labor every day
without complaint,
pay the mortgage promptly,
visit my mother-in-law on schedule,
do most of the shopping,
occasional laundry,
the dishes, now and then,
work in the yard,
around the house,
ignore other women,
ferry my daughter back and forth as asked,
walk the dog faithfully,
clean the garage,
nevertheless,
I have bad breath.

. . . something else to work on.

Developmental Disorder

William's feet refuse to reach the ground,
a problem
which makes walking hard,
flying
easy.

Foreshortening

William awakens to morning again,
regards the rooftops of 114th Street and hollers "Shit!
This isn't Italy,
the Renaissance."
Soon enough, he finds himself reminded
that neither is he Michelangelo.

Inventory

one suit (unworn)
three wives (total)
two jobs (current)
eleven Franco Corelli CDs (some rare)
four dress shirts (blue)
two Subarus (unwashed)
three pair of sweats (also unwashed)
two kids (adult)
one mortgage (oppressive)
one checking account (flat)
one liver (extra-large)

Late Theological Regret

On the question of God,
William wavers.

If one exists,
who should go first,
say what?

God does not add much to William's cosmology,
only leaves him something else to explain,
one more relationship with which to deal.

May has come again
and gone;
William observes.
The plants whose names he promises to learn
have faithfully survived another frost
in this, his fifty-seventh year.

Morning lights the kitchen.
The children have gone off to school,
and William finds himself sipping coffee,
quite unexpectedly,
with her who shares his soul.

For that moment
and moments such as that,
William has nowhere to give thanks.

Mistake

Inspired by life's possibilities,
but ever in need of guidance,
William followed literature's great heroes
and grabbed life by the balls,
firmly,
as suggested,
for which familiarity life,
immediately and forever,
predictably,
kicked him shitless.

Of William's Parts
(after Brautigan)

At William's age,
wrong parts harden —
the arteries, for example.
What woman looks at those?

. . . no matter a brave frame,
perfect posture,
a silver mane,
or eyes that read the heart,
the poet's soul.

Women claim to be understanding,
but William still hears them whisper,
" . . . hard, but in the wrong parts."

On Immortality

The photographs,
in faded sienna,
show men in serious suits,
women in black,
their hair pulled back,
solemn,
a boy in curls and frills
and a girl soldier-straight,
ankles touching,
looking a generation older than her age.
Should I know these people?
Did they always seem so unforgiving?

Someday,
someone may find a photograph of me,
not in a dusty box,
ignored in some closet,
but on a computer,
one among a gallery of forms and faces,
forever in vivid color,
in a world where only memory fades.
Someday,
someone may take a look at me and ask:
Should I know him?
Did he always sit with his feet up,
holding a beer,
laughing?

Waiting For Word

William sits above the Hudson with a six-pack,
his feet too sad to move,
counting fly shit on the window,
watching vultures circle.

He sits there well.
Like Cousin Jack, who makes the best spaghetti sauce with crabs
in Columbia, Maryland,
everyone has a gift.
William has the gift of heightened disappointment.
Anything can ruin his afternoon.
He knows where the strongest buildings buckle,
when summer's brightest day begins to fail.

Psychiatrists would medicate for reasons of illness,
playwrights pull the curtain for lack of tragedy.

But William knows what's real and all his own
as he sits there,
sucks a beer and watches
while the sun collapses slowing
into Jersey.

EPILOGUE

. . . and Epilogue

Anyone who failed to read these words for laughs
will better know the score
when, in half-light growing dimmer,
he trips upon
his own
last line.

WILLIAM CIPRIANO

William Cipriano (1938 – 2021) got his BA, MA, MSW, and Ed.D. from Columbia University. He studied opera at The Julliard School of New York and earned his LCSW-R and multiple credentials in family therapy and supervision from the Mental Health Institute in Palo Alto, California, and from Philadelphia Child Guidance.

He was Program Coordinator of Child and Adolescent Services, Outpatient, at St. Vincent's Hospital Westchester and Adjunct Associate Professor in the Graduate School of Education at Lehman College in the Bronx, NY.

In earlier years, he was a translator for United States Army Intelligence in Germany during the Berlin Wall crisis of the 1960s, a tenor in New York operas, a journalist in Montreal, Canada, and an English professor and theater director at the University of Würzburg, Germany.

From his college years until the end of his life, Bill wrote poems and stories. He brought his many skills to bear in his clinical work and his teaching and training of school counselors and family therapists. At home, he continued to sing and entertain, providing family and friends with laughter and love, wisdom and wit, music and song.